THE **DK** POCKET GUIDE TO

GOLF

PRACTICE DRILLS

THE 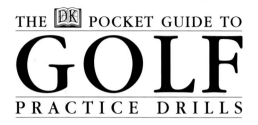 POCKET GUIDE TO
GOLF
PRACTICE DRILLS

PETER BALLINGALL

PHOTOGRAPHY BY
STEVEN BARTHOLOMEW

DORLING KINDERSLEY

LONDON • NEW YORK • STUTTGART • MOSCOW

A Dorling Kindersley Book

MANAGING EDITOR Francis Ritter
MANAGING ART EDITOR Gillian Allan

Produced for Dorling Kindersley by
Bob Gordon Design and Spider Books, London

First published in Great Britain in 1995 by
Dorling Kindersley Limited, 9 Henrietta Street,
London WC2E 8PS

Reprinted 1996

Visit us on the World Wide Web at
http://www.dk.com

A CIP catalogue record for this book is available from
the British Library.

ISBN 0-7513-0245-7

Reproduced by Euroscan
Printed in Hong Kong by Wing King Tong Co Ltd.

FOREWORD

There have been many teachers throughout the history of golf but there have been very few great teachers. Peter Ballingall is one of that rare breed because he is one of the game's great communicators. His approach to teaching is both simple and straightforward but, much more importantly, it works because of his rare gift of easy communication.

In this unique and stylish volume Peter has gathered together sound advice on good golfing methods and a collection of practice drills that are both invaluable and instantly accessible. I thoroughly commend it to you. It will never be far from my side.

MALCOLM CAMPBELL
GOLF MONTHLY

CONTENTS

HOW TO USE THIS BOOK

This book is organized so that it is easy to find the information you want. The book is arranged in three parts: the basic techniques of good golf; 33 practice drills; and sound advice on how to progress. The practice drills are grouped by type of shot (putting, chipping, pitching, full swing, and bunker). Each drill follows a simple format, which is explained on these pages.

LEFT RUNNING HEAD
Shows you which section you have turned to – here, the main section on practice drills and the subsection on putting.

PROBLEM
Helps you spot areas for improvement by pinpointing a difficulty and explaining how it affects play.

DRILL
Gives simple instructions on how to perform a drill that will solve the particular golfing problem described.

FEEL
Focuses on how it feels to play the shot correctly, giving you the confidence to know when you have done well.

BENEFIT
Explains clearly how the drill tackles your problem, and describes the benefit it brings to your game.

PRACTICE DRILLS: PUTTING

PUTTERHEAD DOWN

PROBLEM Do you hit the ball off-target and find that your stroke is not smooth? This is because your wrists are active during the stroke.

Hinge wrists and clubhead upwards

DRILL Hold out the putter in front of you, and hinge the wrists so that the clubhead rises upwards. Now lower the clubhead downwards as far as it will go. Notice how the wrists have become arched. Adopt a putting stance, keeping the putterhead down. Make some putts with the putterhead down in both the backswing and throughswing.

FEEL The wrists feel as though they are in splints. They are no longer able to flick the putterhead at the ball. The stroke seems to be made by the shoulders instead of the hands.

Stand with an outstretched

BENEFIT You learn to keep your wrists inactive so that your shoulders give the stroke a smoother rhythm and a sweeter contact with the ball for greater accuracy.

50

STEP-BY-STEP ILLUSTRATIONS
Clear and easy-to-follow photographs and artworks support the text and make the drills simple to practise.

KEY

Guide to visual devices used in this book.

Yellow balls are hit; orange not

Shows incorrect play

Shows direction

Shows swing movement

Shows body position

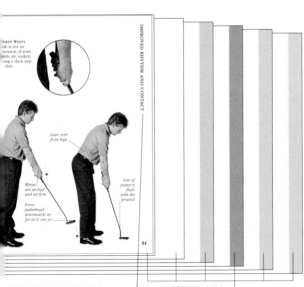

SUNKEN WRISTS
*...lub is not an
...tension of arms.
...rists are sunken,
...ring a slack grip
club.*

IMPROVED RHYTHM AND CONTACT

Lean over from hips

Wrists are arched and set firm

Force putterhead downwards as far as it can go

Sole of putter is flush with the ground

51

RIGHT RUNNING HEAD
In the drills section, gives simple description of each drill's benefit. In sections one and three, gives spread title.

TINT BANDS
Pages are colour coded for easy access. Colours are matched on the contents page and in the shirt colour in each section.

9

INTRODUCTION

All aspiring golfers wish to have good ball control as well as a golf swing that really looks good. While wishing for these is one thing, working hard to achieve them is another. You alone can do that. Finding a qualified teacher is a good start, but what matters is how you use your teacher's information to develop your own mastery of the game.

CONFIDENCE AND COMPETENCE

This book has two aims: to help you improve your technique and develop a 'muscle memory' of how it feels to play a successful shot. Both are indispensable aspects of learning to play golf confidently and competently.

Too many tips serve only to confuse; everything included in this book has the single purpose of improving your actions into, and through the ball. To start with, I take you through the essentials of good golf – how to stand correctly, grip the club, transfer your weight, and find a sweet rhythm. Then I have selected 33 practice drills to help you improve your game.

HAPPIER AND MORE SUCCESSFUL GOLF

The drills are equally appropriate to the novice and the seasoned golfer. For the beginner they provide a foundation upon which to build; for the more experienced player they offer an opportunity to hone established skills. I hope that this book will lead you, whatever your level of experience, to happier and more successful golf.

PETER BALLINGALL

CHOOSING PRACTICE DRILLS

There are three reasons why you may
play poor golf: confusion about what
to do; doubts and uncertainties about
the outcome; and misalignment in the
address position. You may know
what to do but don't believe it will
happen this time; you may know
what to do but set up inappropriately.

Either problem spoils your success.
This gnaws at your self-belief and
leads to your doubting your ability.
So you then try hard. This leads
to tightness, which promotes
errors and leads to further doubts
next time around. These drills are
designed to clear your mind and
help you get off this carousel.

GOOD TECHNIQUE
*All the drills help you to
develop control of the
ball by helping you to
understand the essential
geometry of clubface
alignment, swingpath,
and plane.*

THE PRACTICE DRILLS

This book contains a collection of 33 practice drills – simple but highly effective ways of improving your technique. Some have been in existence for a long time and are adapted from other teachers. Others I have devised myself in the course of my career as a professional teacher of the game.

OUT OF BALANCE
The drills teach you about balance, weight transfer, and the centrifugal forces found in all good swings.

CHOPPING LOGS
If you heave the club as though chopping logs, learn that power comes from an elasticity of movement that creates speed through impact.

FINDING A DRILL

The drills are grouped into different types of shot – putting, chipping, pitching, full swing, and bunker play. To start with, choose one area of your game on which to concentrate. Then look at the drills in your chosen section. Each works on a particular element of the shot. Choose one that focuses on your problem and that appeals to your imagination.

13

USING PRACTICE DRILLS

Resist the temptation to flit, butterfly fashion, between a large number of drills. Practise the drills one at a time until you have mastered each one. Understanding the aim of each drill is important. So too is understanding why it will help. A third crucial element is to become fully aware of the feel of your actions. Intellectualize (learn the 'how'); conceptualize (understand the 'why'); then react (experience the 'feeling').

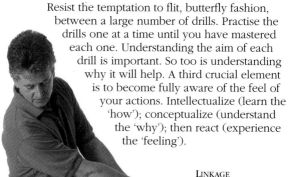

LINKAGE
Be aware of your hands in front of your torso into, through, and just after impact.

UNDERSTANDING WHY
What your mind can perceive your body can achieve. Not until you understand the 'how' and the 'why' will your game improve. The style of your swing is quite unimportant: control of the ball is what counts.

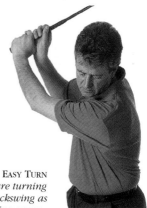

EASY TURN
Feel that you are turning easily in the backswing as though conserving energy.

CREATE GOOD HABITS

Be mindful of how your body feels as you execute each drill. When you do something different it feels strange at first. Do not be nervous about this. Hold a position as you perform your drill and observe how it feels so that you can recognize it next time. Repetition of the good things creates good habits.

SMOOTH MOVE
A powerful swing begins in the feet, so feel that the arms swing down at the same time as your weight transfers.

HOW TO PRACTISE

Practice does not make perfect: it makes permanent. So if you practise incorrectly you will be permanently wrong. Perfect practice makes perfect. Therefore, the key is to practise intelligently.

SHORT AND SWEET Short and frequent practice sessions are more beneficial than isolated, lengthy ones. If you apply yourself to one or two drills for five minutes a day, every day for a month, you will become expert at them. You will understand how they will transform your game and you will establish a lasting muscle memory. The movements will become habitual and will come through in your golf swing without the need for conscious thought.

SLOW MOTION Practise each drill in slow motion until you are confident of the moves and feel comfortable with them. Then build up your speed slowly until you are making successful shots at full speed.

BE PATIENT It takes a little time for new habits to become established. The rewards, however, are well worth the wait.

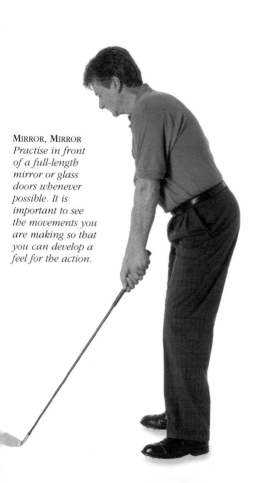

MIRROR, MIRROR
*Practise in front
of a full-length
mirror or glass
doors whenever
possible. It is
important to see
the movements you
are making so that
you can develop a
feel for the action.*

MENTAL PRACTICE

Every golfer admits that golf is played in the mind. Opinions vary about the extent to which the mind affects play. Some say that golf is 90 per cent mental, others that it is less so. All agree, however, that the mental aspects of golf make up considerably more than half of the skills necessary in order to play the game to a high level.

Understanding the technical skills is of little use without appreciating how to improve the mental skills. Self-improvement begins only when you recognize the powers of concentration, visualization, and rational thought.

CONCENTRATION This is the art of focusing attention on one thing to the exclusion of all else. As you perform your drills, become absorbed in what you are doing and in how it feels physically; that is, be 'mindful', not 'thoughtful'.

VISUALIZATION Visualization is practised by all good golfers and forms the basis of your progress. It is the art of putting onto your internal movie screen an image that depicts and predicts success.

Visualizing a successful shot is easy when you ask this question before playing any shot: 'What do I want the ball to do?' As you survey the target your imagination will create pictures of the ball flying through the air and landing in the target zone. It will show you everything in detail: the weight of the shot, the direction of flight, and the roll of the ball.

The mind becomes peaceful and relaxed as it engages with the target in this way and enables the brain to 'react' more confidently and competently. When practising a drill, use your imagination to 'see' the effect it will have on your performance. By seeing its value the brain will send the appropriate messages to the muscles and organs of the body to accomplish that drill effectively.

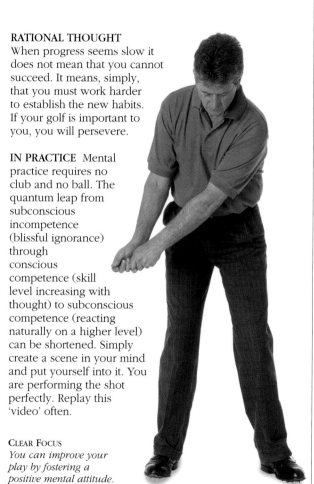

RATIONAL THOUGHT

When progress seems slow it does not mean that you cannot succeed. It means, simply, that you must work harder to establish the new habits. If your golf is important to you, you will persevere.

IN PRACTICE Mental practice requires no club and no ball. The quantum leap from subconscious incompetence (blissful ignorance) through conscious competence (skill level increasing with thought) to subconscious competence (reacting naturally on a higher level) can be shortened. Simply create a scene in your mind and put yourself into it. You are performing the shot perfectly. Replay this 'video' often.

CLEAR FOCUS
You can improve your play by fostering a positive mental attitude.

19

Basic
Techniques

The first step to improving your golf technique is to have a sound understanding of the golf swing and a good set-up routine.

THE GOLF SWING

Everyone possesses a natural style of golf swing. History has taught that no two champions ever swung the club alike: individual style has played a role in their success. History has also taught, however, that all great players do something similar in, to, and through the hitting area. It is in this area of the golf swing that control of the ball is to be found.

Upper body and arms move back together

Body is comfortably positioned, ready for action

FLOWING ACTION The golf swing is essentially a flowing action of the arms, hands, and body interacting independently but in synchronization with each other from a semi-stationary start to a balanced finish. It is a rhythmical, 'elastic' movement – not a series of contortions.

While the arms do swing the club, the powerhouse of the golf swing is the body. The energy is created through its rotations and the transfer of weight.

Once you are clear about how the simple geometry of swing will give you control of the ball, your actions from beginning to finish must be naturally coordinated. This can happen only when you stop trying too hard or thinking too much about what you are doing.

Arms swing freely down and through

Lower body rotates in forward swing

Weight transfers

23

PROPERTIES OF THE SWING

Understanding the properties of the swing is important to help you form the foundations of a good swing and therefore of a successful game.

THE PENDULUM Picture the pendulum of a grandfather clock swinging in a smooth, rhythmical, and unhurried way. It is suspended by a chain from a hub, or axis, in the clock face, forming a radius. This makes the pendulum move in the shape of an arc.

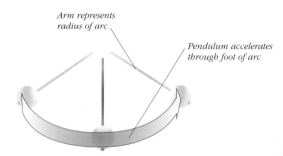

Arm represents radius of arc

Pendulum accelerates through foot of arc

When the pendulum swings from left to right, the beginning of the arc seems to begin at an easy pace and gather momentum through the foot of the arc. Then, the start of the arc from right to left once again starts at the same easy pace. The pendulum may swing either fast or slow. The swing is natural and uninhibited: no external force is applied.

THE HUMAN PENDULUM Now translate this action to golf. The base of the neck is the hub, which remains still throughout the swing. The arms are the chain; they maintain a relatively wide radius as they swing the club freely and naturally from one side to another.

The beginning of the forward swing of the clubhead begins at the same easy pace as the beginning of the backswing, although it accelerates through the foot of the arc. The swing is unhurried. There is no aggression or applied physical force.

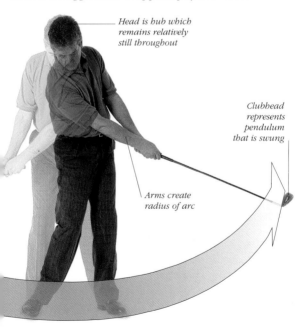

Head is hub which remains relatively still throughout

Clubhead represents pendulum that is swung

Arms create radius of arc

RHYTHM, TEMPO, AND TIMING

Rhythm, tempo, and timing are fundamentals of a good swing action.

RHYTHM Rhythm is a swing with a beat. In golf, the start of the downswing begins at the same pace as the start of the backswing.

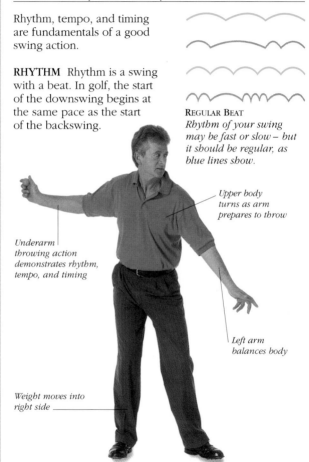

REGULAR BEAT
Rhythm of your swing may be fast or slow – but it should be regular, as blue lines show.

Upper body turns as arm prepares to throw

Underarm throwing action demonstrates rhythm, tempo, and timing

Left arm balances body

Weight moves into right side

TEMPO Tempo refers to the speed of the swing. A golf swing can be fast or slow – either is satisfactory as long as it has a regular rhythm. Find a speed for your swing that suits you. Don't be frightened of experimenting.

Action is coordinated and balanced

MARKING TIME
Metronome marks out regular beat at speed of your choosing.

Body turns to face target

Weight transfers

TIMING Timing describes how the movements of the body coordinate during the swing action. The movements of the hands and arms synchronize with those of the major muscle groups of the upper and lower body.

Perfect timing is perfect coordination. It occurs when the arms and hands swing the club down, to, and through the ball in time with the transfer of weight and turn of the body to the target.

27

CENTRIFUGAL FORCE

Centrifugal force is an energy that emanates outwards directly from a rotational centre. In almost every sport where something is thrown or hit with a bat, centrifugal forces are in action when power is required. The discus thrower, baseball pitcher, and tennis player all achieve their power through the transfer of weight and rotations of the major muscle groups of the body, which fuel the smaller muscles of the hands and arms.

THE POWER OF THE GOLF SWING In golf, distance is achieved when the clubhead travels in an arc that brushes with the ball-to-target line, and when its clubface is square to that swingpath through impact. For the clubhead to travel at optimum speed through this point, the force comes not from the hands or arms but from the turns of the body.

Upper body turns as arms swing racket back

Weight moves onto right foot

Upper body turns to coil body like a spring

Picture skaters on an ice-rink, arms linked to form a chain. The skater on the outside is skated faster than he could skate solo, moved by the energy emanating from the person in the centre who simply turns on the spot.

Hips and midriff rotate

Left heel comes off ground as weight moves onto right foot

Right knee moves around towards target

So it is with the clubface. It responds to the energies emanating from the feet up through the body as it turns and down through the arms and into the club shaft. This creates top speed, and thus power, distance, and control.

Feet transfer weight and right foot ends on toe with heel looking to rear

29

WEIGHT TRANSFER

Balance is fundamental to an efficient and consistent golf swing. So too is weight transfer. As long as your golf swing is contained within the balance of your stance you can achieve both good transfer of weight and power from your swing.

ADDRESS
Feet, knees, hips, and shoulders all support each other at address.

BALANCE POINTS
The point of balance moves into the right side in the backswing, and then into the left during the throughswing. The joints in the body that give balance are the feet, knees, hips, and shoulders. These parts of the body must always support each other – at address, in the backswing, and at the end of the throughswing.

EQUAL SCALES
For medium irons, weight is distributed equally at address.

BACKSWING
Weight is on right, with right foot, knee, hips, and shoulders in line.

THROUGHSWING
Weight transfers to left side, left foot, knee, hip, and shoulders balanced and in line.

WEIGHTED RIGHT
Majority of bodyweight is on right side in backswing.

WEIGHTED LEFT
Left foot, knee, and hip take most of weight at finish.

THE SET-UP

The set-up at address is crucial to good,
consistent play. Golf has been described
as 98 per cent set-up and 2 per cent start.
It is important to be clear in your mind
about the techniques of playing a shot.
It is also vital that you believe you can
succeed. But neither of these elements
will ensure your success if you set up
inappropriately at the beginning.

Grip, alignment, stance, and posture –
GASP – are the fundamental aspects of
good set-up. They are described in
detail on the following pages.

RELEVANCE OF GOOD SET-UP When
practising or playing golf you are literally
setting everything up for a reaction to take
place. You have selected your target and
chosen a club. You should have a clear
mental vision of how the ball is going to
fly and roll. You have subconsciously, or
consciously, gathered information on wind
conditions, the lie of the ball, and the
contours of the fairway or the speed of the
green. All these elements have been taken
in through your senses. Once you have
assimilated this information you simply
move into position and react to it.

Every part of you that is above the line
of the shaft at address should feel passive:
hands, arms, stomach, shoulders, and
facial muscles. Everything below that line
should feel springy: feet, knees, and legs.
Pay attention to feeling this way.

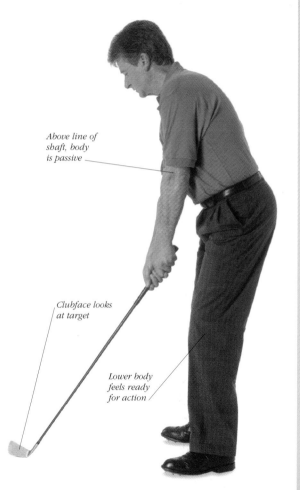

Above line of shaft, body is passive

Clubface looks at target

Lower body feels ready for action

GRIP

The single purpose of the golf swing is to present the club face squarely to the target at, and through, impact. The hands connect the club face to the power source of the golf swing action. The world's greatest players agree that the hands control the club face and that their grip gives them control of the ball.

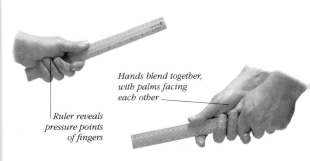

Hands blend together, with palms facing each other

Ruler reveals pressure points of fingers

HOLDING THE CLUB The palms must face each other on the grip in order to act as one unit. They must blend together and with the grip in a light but secure way so that they naturally deliver the club face squarely to the target at impact every time.

Taking hold of a ruler will teach you about the pressure points of the fingers. Feel those same pressure points as you take hold of the club. Avoid holding the grip tightly: tension will transmit through your arms and shoulders, making a free swing impossible to achieve.

VARDON GRIP
*Smallest finger
of right hand
overlaps second
finger of left hand
underneath.*

INTERLOCKING GRIP
*Smallest finger
of right hand
interlocks with
index finger of
left hand.*

BASEBALL GRIP
*Hands are placed
right below left on
handle.*

ADAPTING THE GRIP You may
adapt your grip, using the Vardon,
interlocking, or baseball method, to
suit your individual style of play. Find
the best style for you.

An old golfing adage says, 'If the
ball bends to the left – move both
hands to the left on the handle. If
the ball bends to the right – move
both hands to the right'. This
adjustment resets the clubface
alignment at impact and the direction
of its swingpath through the ball.

HAND POSITION
*V-shape of right
hand points to
right ear. V-shape
of left hand points
to right shoulder.*

35

ALIGNMENT

Clubface alignment and body alignment at address are fundamental to attaining control of the ball. The ball always ends up in the direction in which the clubface was looking at impact, so align it squarely to the target at the start. The swingpath of the clubhead is determined by the alignment of the shoulders, hips, knees, and feet, so align them parallel with the ball-to-target line at address for the ball to fly straight.

TAKING GOOD AIM

Aiming yourself towards the target is the one thing *not* to do if you wish the ball to fly straight to your target. Imagine that you are standing on one line of a railway track with the ball in front of you on the other track. The clubface looks directly down the track that runs to the target. Although it appears that the railway lines meet on the horizon, they do not: they remain parallel to one another.

SQUARE STANCE
Clubface points to target with body parallel to target line.

Align your stance parallel with the target but to the left of it. Remember that the arc of the swing brushes with the ball-to-target line on a tangent 'inside-square-to-inside' (see page 90). If the swingpath crosses the target line from either the inside or the outside, the ball will not go to the target. This geometry is useful when you wish to correct a fault or to hit the ball with intentional 'draw' or 'fade', altering the ball's line of flight.

CLOSED STANCE
Clubface is square with body aligned to right for hook.

OPEN STANCE
Clubface is square with body aligned to left for slice.

STANCE AND BALL POSITION

The design of the club determines where the ball sits in relation to your feet at address. Here is a simple way of getting it right every time.

HOLD IT, AIM IT, FACE IT Firstly, take hold of the club with your arms extended in front of you. Secondly, keeping both hands on the handle, lean over with your right foot forward to place and aim the clubface behind the ball.

HOLD IT
Hold out arms in front of you to check clubface alignment.

Thirdly, keeping both hands on the handle and the club in position, align feet, knees, hips, and shoulders parallel to the ball-to-target line. For all clubs, the feet remain a comfortable shoulder-width apart for perfect balance.

This routine has two benefits: you will find a self-regulated distance to stand from the ball with any club; the ball will find its own position relative to your feet.

RELATIVE PLACEMENT
For driver, ball is near left heel; for mid-iron, between centre of stance and left heel; for lofted iron, it is in centre of stance.

AIM IT
Lean over from hips and onto right foot to align clubface square to target.

FACE IT
Align body parallel to ball-to-target line without moving club.

POSTURE

Good posture is essential. The plane of the swing, the direction of the swingpath, and alignment at impact are all influenced by the way you stand at the start.

The ideal posture is of straight lines and angles. Lean over from the hips – never the waist. This keeps the lower spine straight, letting the hands and arms hang down freely below the chin. It also promotes balance – an important requirement. When the lower spine is straight, the body can turn easily both ways without changing the angle of tilt of the spine, and therefore the swingplane.

SIDE TO SIDE
Gap between heels is hip-width, giving sideways balance.

FRONT TO BACK
Head in front balances bottom out behind.

UP AND DOWN
Weight is supported from hips down, creating balance.

THREE-DIMENSIONAL BALANCE

Placing the feet a comfortable width apart creates balance from side to side. Leaning the head over (but with the chin up) counterbalances the bottom, which sticks out a little, creating balance from front to back. The bulk of the bodyweight is supported by the feet, knees, and hips, creating balance up and down. Never do anything in your golf swing that will interfere with this balance.

The posture alters slightly as you change from the driver to a wedge. You stand a little taller for the driver and are more over the ball for a wedge. Yet the principles of balance remain.

UNIVERSAL PRINCIPLES
Principles of balance remain whatever club you are using.

HEAD POSITION

'Keep your head down, and keep it still', is possibly the most misunderstood command in golf. The thing to do is to keep your chin *up*. How can you make a full turn for a powerful swing when your chin is buried on your chest? The ideal head position is attained when raising your eyes without lifting your head lets you see the horizon, and lowering your eyes lets you see the ball.

On putts, chips, and all other shots that do not require power, the head must remain still throughout the stroke. On all full golf swings, the head must be allowed to move. It rotates a little on the backswing and throughswing; moves slightly to the right as the upper body coils; and moves back as the weight transfers into the impact area. But it must move neither ahead of the ball before contact is made nor up and down. Try the exercise illustrated here.

Amateurs try hard to keep their head still on the power shots, thereby stifling all natural mobility. They then allow the head to waggle loosely on the short shots that need accuracy.

FACING FRONT
Make mark on mirror so that reflection is opposite your throat.

RIGHT TURN
*When turning to right,
mark is reflected
against back of neck.*

LEFT TURN
*Mark shows against
back of neck in swing
to other side.*

43

PRACTICE DRILLS

*The second step to good golf is to
understand which areas of your
game need improvement and to
work on them single-mindedly.*

PUTTING DRILLS

Putting has often been referred to as a science all on its own. Over the ages, golfers have developed different ways of holding the club and have created putters of every possible design.

Conventional right hand below left method

Broom handle method

The putting stroke is a pendulum action where the movement of the clubhead is created by a gentle rocking action of the shoulders (see pages 24–5). The hands lead the clubface through the ball; the clubface 'collects' the ball rather than hits it. Putting is easiest when the hands and wrists do nothing.

There are several methods used by great players to eliminate the wristy flick: the conventional right hand below left; the broom handle; the left hand below right; the Langer; and the conventional 'reverse overlap', with the left forefinger pressing against the fingers of the right hand. Experiment until you find a method that suits you.

The putting drills will help you to control the club and ball; eliminate use of the wrists; and synchronize the movements between arms, shoulders, and hands to produce a sound, repetitive action. Also vitally important is the need to believe that your putts will go in.

Left hand below right method

Langer method

Conventional 'reverse overlap' method

47

FINGER PRESS

PROBLEM Do you have difficulty in gauging the distance to the target and miss your putts to the left of the hole? If so, you are flicking the putterhead at the ball with your wrists.

DRILL Hold the putter with the left forefinger overlapping the third finger of the right hand. Address the ball, pressing the left forefinger against the fingers of the right hand. Notice how the putterhead moves backwards a little. Make sure that the hands sit over the ball. Maintain the pressure as you make your stroke. The right wrist maintains its position throughout.

Hands sit in advance of putterhead

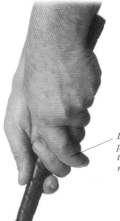

Left forefinger presses against third finger of right hand

FEEL The action feels more compact. The back of the left hand seems to lead the putterhead. You feel that the ball is collected by the putter – there is no sensation of hit.

BENEFIT The clubface looks squarely to the target through impact, which improves accuracy. You have more control of the roll of the ball.

Pressing forefinger makes clubhead move backwards

Hands remain in advance of putterhead through impact

PUTTERHEAD DOWN

PROBLEM Do you hit the ball off-target and find that your stroke is not smooth? This is because your wrists are active during the stroke.

DRILL Hold out the putter in front of you, and hinge the wrists so that the clubhead rises upwards. Now lower the clubhead downwards as far as it will go. Notice how the wrists have become arched. Adopt a putting stance, keeping the putterhead down. Make some putts with the putterhead down in both the backswing and throughswing.

FEEL The wrists feel as though they are in splints. They are no longer able to flick the putterhead at the ball. The stroke seems to be made by the shoulders instead of the hands.

BENEFIT You learn to keep your wrists inactive so that your shoulders give the stroke a smoother rhythm and a sweeter contact with the ball for greater accuracy.

Hinge wrists and clubhead upwards

Stand tall with arms outstretched

SUNKEN WRISTS
Club is not an extension of arms. Wrists are sunken, giving a slack grip on club.

Lean over from hips

Wrists are arched and set firm

Force putterhead downwards as far as it can go

Sole of putter is flush with the ground

51

BOOK DRILL

PROBLEM Do you slice your putts, leaving them short and to the right of the hole, or pulled to the left? Your arms, shoulders, and wrists may be out of synchronization, causing you to lift the putter in the takeaway and swing it off line.

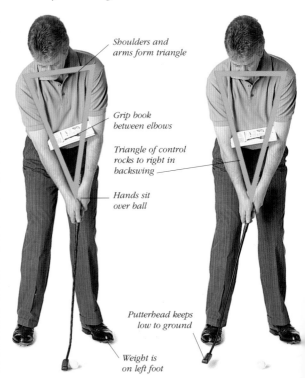

Shoulders and arms form triangle

Grip book between elbows

Triangle of control rocks to right in backswing

Hands sit over ball

Putterhead keeps low to ground

Weight is on left foot

DRILL Support a medium-sized book between your elbows. Make your stroke without letting the book slip. If you practise in front of a mirror you will see how the shoulders and arms move as one, creating a triangle of control.

Triangle of control rocks to left as stroke is made

Firm wrists lead clubhead

Putterhead collects ball on upswing

FEEL The stroke feels compact and secure. You feel a gentle rocking movement of the shoulders.

BENEFIT Gripping a book helps to establish a sense of your arms, shoulders, and wrists moving as one unit. This moves the clubhead through a shallow arc, creating top-spin and a more accurate roll to the target.

53

ONE-THIRD: TWO-THIRDS

PROBLEM Do your putts end up either longer or shorter than you intended? This may be because your backswing is too large. This slows the clubhead through impact, which makes it difficult to gauge the pace of the putt.

DRILL Place a ball opposite the right foot and another one (the object ball) just inside the left heel. Place the clubhead between the balls and play the object ball without touching the other one.

FEEL You feel the shoulders rock a small way back and a longer way through the stroke. The smooth rhythm of the rocking action makes the clubhead seem to collect the ball as it passes.

BENEFIT By giving the stroke a one-third: two-thirds ratio – taking the clubhead one-third back in the backswing and two-thirds forward in the throughswing – the clubhead accelerates through impact. This gives the putt the correct pace to take the ball to target.

Weight favours left side

Take up position to play yellow ball

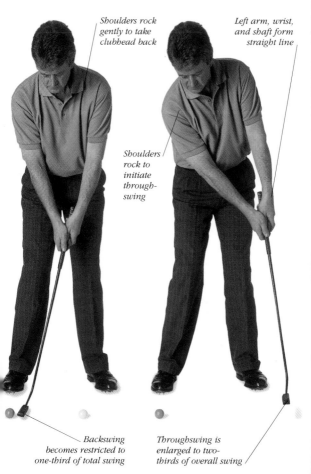

Shoulders rock gently to take clubhead back

Left arm, wrist, and shaft form straight line

Shoulders rock to initiate through-swing

Backswing becomes restricted to one-third of total swing

Throughswing is enlarged to two-thirds of overall swing

Two-club Channel

PROBLEM Do you miss putts when you are sure you are reading the line to target accurately? This could be caused by a poor swingpath through impact.

DRILL Place two clubs on the ground to form a channel only slightly wider than the width of the putterhead, and pointing to the target. Place a ball between the clubs and make the putt, ensuring that the clubhead moves through the ball and along the channel.

FEEL On short putts you feel the putter move straight back from the ball. On longer ones the head tracks on a more obvious arc, but still within the channel. Feel the left shoulder lead the putter to the target.

BENEFIT You learn to allow the putter to track on a slight arc inside the ball-to-target line in the backswing and then straight through to the target in the forward swing. This gives you greater accuracy.

Stand tall, leaning over from hips, with eyes over ball

End of club is opposite right foot

Channel is slightly wider than putterhead

56

EXTENDED BACKSWING
A backswing that is too long would extend beyond channel.

Short backswing is contained within channel

Clubhead tracks marginally on inside in backswing

Swingpath of putter goes down channel directly towards target

MIRROR DRILL

PROBLEM Anxiety about holing or missing a putt often results in the eyes and head coming up too early to see what has happened. This drags the ball off line as the shoulders pull the club to the left.

DRILL Place a ball on top of a small mirror. Take up the address position so that you see the reflection of your eyes in the mirror. Notice that your eyes sit parallel with the top and bottom edges of the mirror; this means that your shoulders are parallel with the ball-to-target line. Make your putting stroke. Keep looking at the reflection of your eyes until long after the ball has gone.

FEEL You feel the right shoulder move more under the chin than around it. The left arm, hand, and putter seem to separate from the left side of the body as the club moves directly towards the target.

Take up address with ball on top of mirror

Head remains motionless throughout stroke

BENEFIT Focusing your eyes on the mirror keeps your body facing the ball-to-target line throughout the shot. This gives you a correct swingpath and sends the ball to the target.

Eyes are parallel with top and bottom edges of mirror

Eyes still look at mirror after ball has gone

Clubface has collected ball

EYES CLOSED

PROBLEM Do you try too hard to get things right? The eyes often play tricks on you and affect your stroke if you do not also use other senses in playing a shot.

DRILL With the eyes open, assess where the hole is and how much of an action will be needed to make the ball reach the hole. Then close your eyes and make the stroke.

Before opening your eyes, assess where the ball has finished in relation to the target. You may be wildly inaccurate at first but in a short time will amaze yourself with your accuracy.

FEEL Your feel for pace and the rhythm of your action becomes more acute. Your mind becomes peacefully focused as it experiences the flow of the movement.

BENEFIT When the eyes are closed, other senses come into play and your awareness increases with your feedback of feel. This results in greater relaxation and accuracy.

Take up address position in line with target

With eyes closed, simply react to target

Backswing feels smooth and unhurried

Throughswing is unhurried as you remain focused on target

CHIPPING DRILLS

Even great players miss the green on occasion – but all can chip the ball close to the hole when they do. This removes the pressure from your long game and allows good scores. The object of the chip shot is to fly the ball through the air to the nearest flat surface

Shoulders sit parallel with intended line of flight

Hands are ahead of clubhead and over ball

Weight is firmly on left foot

Clubhead moves through ball, facing target

of the putting green and allow the ball to roll, like a putt, upon landing.

Aim to move the club through the ball as though sending it forwards – not upwards. Make no attempt to get the clubhead under the ball. Keep the hands in advance of the clubhead through impact to enable the loft of the club to deflect the ball upwards and forwards. Only a small swing is needed to propel the ball to the nearest flat surface. The ball rolls a little with a lofted club, further with a less lofted one.

Hands lead clubhead into and through ball

Stance may be slightly open to target line

Weight favours forward foot

BUTT OF HANDLE TO WRIST

PROBLEM When chipping, does the ball shoot along the ground a long way past the hole? If so, this is because you are trying to scoop the clubface under the ball with the wrists to get it airborne, and in so doing contact the ball on the upswing.

DRILL Secure the end of the handle to the left wrist using a wrist band. Make the shot, keeping the handle snug into the wrist. Brush the grass as you swing through.

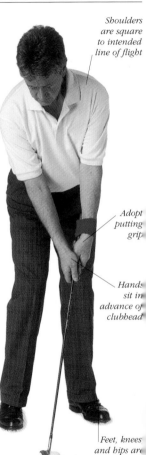

Shoulders are square to intended line of flight

Adopt putting grip

Hands sit in advance of clubhead

Feet, knees and hips are slightly open

Tuck butt of handle into wrist band

Hold club farther down shaft than usual

FEEL The left arm draws the club away in the backswing, keeping the clubhead near the ground. The forward swing begins with weight transfer to the left; the right knee folds in towards the target; the hips open to allow the arms, hands, and clubhead to pass through the ball.

Arms retain triangle with shoulders

Butt of handle is still snug against wrist

Back of wrist leads clubhead

BENEFIT The arms and hands go through the ball ahead of the clubhead and the ball rises of its own accord as the clubface passes through it. This results in flying chip shots.

Right knee folds inwards to target

Clubhead has collected ball

TWO AT ONCE

PROBLEM Do you stub the ground in front of the ball when chipping? A wristy flick is usually to blame, catching the ball on the upswing and skimming it across the green to the rough on the other side.

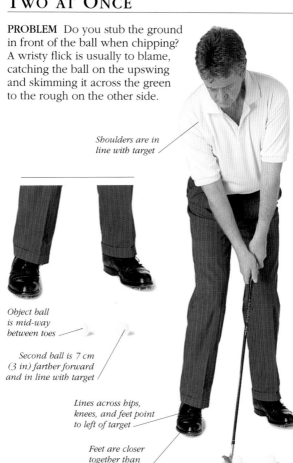

Shoulders are in line with target

Object ball is mid-way between toes

Second ball is 7 cm (3 in) farther forward and in line with target

Lines across hips, knees, and feet point to left of target

Feet are closer together than for a full shot

DRILL Adopt the usual stance, with the object ball opposite your nose, and your eyes parallel to the ball-to-target line. The ball appears to be in the middle of the stance. Place another ball about 7 cm (3 in) to the left of the first ball, in line with the target. Focus on contacting both balls with one swing. Once you have hit the first ball, continue your swing to hit the second one. The first will have popped up and will be on its way.

FEEL The swing feels longer and shallower than before. The arms seem to separate from the body and extend towards the target. The clubhead lags behind the hands, staying low through the ball.

BENEFIT By extending your swing you will make pure, crisp contact with the ball, which will fly through the air towards the target.

Hips turn, right knee folds towards target, right heel comes out of ground

First ball flies over second ball, towards target

PUTT IT

PUTT IT

PROBLEM Do you find it difficult to stop flicking your wrists? When this happens, your club scuffs the ground or clips the ball on the upswing.

DRILL Using a No. 7 or 8 iron, set up as for putting, with your body aligned with the ball-to-target line. Hold the club down the handle using the

Shoulders, hips, knees, and feet are parallel with ball-to-target line

Hold club down handle to approximate length of your putter

Clubface is slightly open

Heel of club is off ground

Clubhead sits on its toe

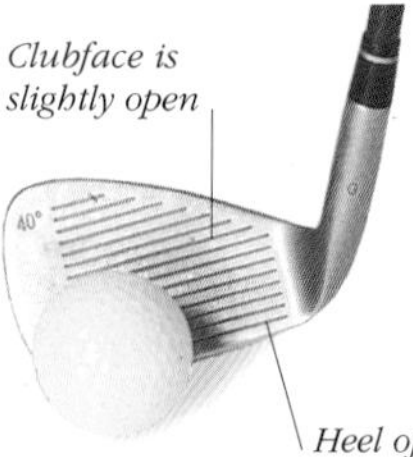

putting grip (see pages 46–7). Arch the wrists so that the clubhead sits on its toe. Place the ball inside the left heel and open the clubface slightly. Putt through the ball, rocking the shoulders gently. Aim to move the ball forwards not upwards.

In putting through ball, hands remain in advance of clubhead

FEEL The hands feel as if they only connect the clubface to the shoulders, which activate the rocking movement. You feel as if the clubhead is collecting rather than hitting the ball.

BENEFIT If you see the shot as nothing more than putting with a lofted putter you will cure your wristy flick and make good chip shots.

69

THE PRO'S APPROACH

PROBLEM Do you prefer to chip with your favourite wedge or other lofted club in every situation but find it hard to control the flight and pace on the ball when rolling it across the green?

DRILL Adopt a slightly open stance but with the shoulders aligned with your intended line of flight and the bodyweight favouring the left side. Place the ball farther back in the

Feet, knees, and hips are aligned slightly to left of target

Weight favours left side

Club moves back, with head close to ground

Position ball farther back in stance than usual

stance than usual. Play the shot mainly with the arms, so that the toe of the club overtakes the heel through impact, creating top-spin.

FEEL The right forearm rotates over the left. The movement is smooth and unhurried. There is a mild inflection of the wrists, although they are only reacting rather than playing a major role.

BENEFIT Rolling the right wrist over the left makes it passive. This results in the ball flying low and rolling farther, as though you were using a less lofted club.

Right forearm overtakes left

Arc of swing is shallow as toe overtakes heel

PITCHING DRILLS

The essence of the pitch shot is to fly the ball high through the air and land it on the green with the minimum of roll. To achieve back-spin on the ball so that it stops quickly requires a crisp downward swing of the arms, with the hands leading the clubhead. The aim is to hit the ball – then the turf.

To attain this, the bodyweight must be firmly on the left side at impact. To make the ball fly high, swing the club down, keeping the right hand inactive. The clubhead

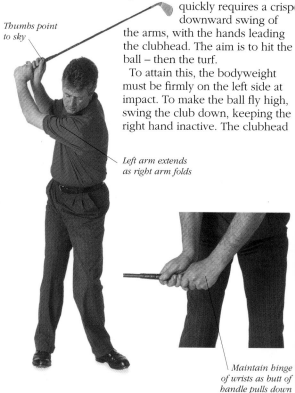

Thumbs point to sky

Left arm extends as right arm folds

Maintain hinge of wrists as butt of handle pulls down

lags behind the hands. Transfer weight in unison with the swing of the arms – and let the club do the rest. Swing the clubhead through the ball as though it were not there. The feet, knees, and hips play their part to initiate the forward swing, although on shorter shots of 40–50 m (40–50 yds) their contribution is small.

Hands lead clubhead into and through ball

Body turns to target at throughswing

Midriff turns to target as arms swing club down

Weight transfers to left side

UMBRELLA SWING

PROBLEM Do you have difficulty in hitting high wedge shots from 60–80 m (60–80 yds) out? Do you 'thin' the ball or hit the ground in front of it? If so, your swingplane is probably too flat.

DRILL Place an umbrella in the ground about 1 m (3 ft) out from your right heel. Make your backswing without knocking over the umbrella. Set the clubface and hinge the wrists early to avoid contact. Turn your shoulders at the same time. Now position the umbrella to the side of your left foot and make some shots without knocking it over.

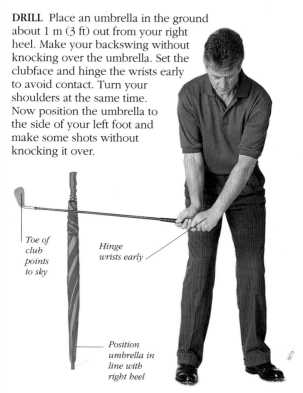

Toe of club points to sky

Hinge wrists early

Position umbrella in line with right heel

FEEL Your wrists seem to hinge the club upwards. Your shoulders feel passive as they turn – they don't tilt. Your arms swing upwards then downwards freely, with the clubhead following.

BENEFIT
The steeper swingplane creates a sharper angle of attack, which generates crisp contact and a high-flying shot that lands softly on the green.

Shoulders turn fully as arms swing upwards

Arms pull butt of handle downwards

Do not make contact with umbrella

TOWEL DRILL

PROBLEM Missing the green from within 50 m (50 yds) damages morale and is costly in terms of your score. The prime cause is poor timing – the arms, legs, and body are out of synchronization.

DRILL Place a towel across your chest and make your swing without letting it slip. As the distance in this instance is quite short, a half swing will suffice. The shoulders turn in the backswing at the same time as the wrists hinge and the arms swing upwards. The bodyweight shifts a little towards the right side.

As the arms swing down, the weight transfers to the left and the midriff rotates to face the target.

FEEL The towel, kept in place by your upper arms, gives you a feeling of confinement. Your arms feel connected to your upper body. Your feet play a much greater role, and they, together with your midriff, fuel the action.

Upper body turns as arms swing upwards

Hands are opposite torso

Grip towel comfortably with upper arms

Weight moves towards right side

BENEFIT Purposefully keeping your arms close to
your body by wrapping a towel around your chest in
this way teaches you to synchronize the movements
of your arms, legs, and body – or the towel would
slip. This allows you to gain both a more authoritative
strike and a crispness of contact with the ball.

*Arms and
body turn
in synch*

*Towel
remains in
position*

*Hands are
in advance
of clubhead*

*Weight is
on left foot*

FULL SWING DRILLS

All the drills explained in this section are devised to improve your swingpath into and through the ball on an arc that travels 'inside-square-to-inside' the ball-to-target line (see page 90).

The drills also help you to recognize and establish a good plane of swing, correct hand action, and power.

Upper body turns fully

Hips turn only a little

Hips rotate

Hands are opposite torso

Weight is on right side

Weight moves in to left side

The drills centre around the four basic positions that are important in golf: the address position; the top of the backswing; the impact position; and the finish. They are grouped in such a way that drills tackling a particular element of the swing are placed together: those that improve hand action; drills to correct swingplane; and drills to encourage better body position.

Torso looks to left

Body is perfectly balanced at finish

Belt buckle faces target

What is equally important to learn is that the whole swing action is greater than the sum of its parts. Good shots won't come until you allow your clubhead to swing through the ball to a full and balanced finish.

Right heel is off ground and looking to rear

Weight is fully on left foot

79

HAND ACTION

PROBLEM Errant shots are the result of the clubface being either closed or open to the target at impact. This is caused by ignorance of how the hands should hinge in the golf swing.

Toe and scorelines of club are looking skywards

Right wrist hinges back on itself and left wrist rotates a little when club reaches hip height

DRILL Hold the club as described on pages 34–35, with the hands blending together lightly but securely. Assume the address position and begin the backswing. Hinge the wrists so that as the club reaches hip height its toe points to the sky. Swing the arms down and present the clubface squarely to the target at impact. Towards the finish, the toe of the club, at hip height, is again looking to the sky.

FEEL The right wrist hinges back on itself and the left rotates a little. At impact the clubhead seems to lag slightly as the back of the left hand looks at the target. You feel a release after impact as the right hand overtakes the left.

BENEFIT Hinging your wrists in the back and forward swing establishes the correct alignment of the clubface in relation to the swingpath and gives greater ball control.

Hands are opposite torso

Back of left hand, palm of right, and clubface are looking at target

Right wrist has overtaken left wrist

Clubhead lags behind hands, arms, and weight shift to collect ball

81

TENNIS RACKET

PROBLEM Simple movements in golf – such as the action of the hands – often appear complicated and unnatural, leading to uncontrolled shots. Seeing how similar movements are made in other sports can clear up confusion and lead to greater control.

Racket face looks to front at hip height as shoulders turn

Back of left hand looks to front

Weight shifts to right side

DRILL Hold a tennis racket as you would a golf club. Make a backswing as though playing a low forehand return with top-spin. At hip height the racket face looks to the front. At impact it looks to the target as your weight shifts to the left. The hands zip the racket over to create top-spin so that, at hip height in the forward swing, the face looks to the rear.

FEEL Feel the natural coordination of the arms, hands, and body turning and moving together as you swing the racket through to the finish. Take note of the way the wrists hinge to work the racket as the upper body turns in the backswing.

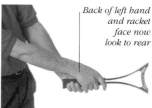

Back of left hand and racket face now look to rear

Right knee folds inwards

Back of left hand and racket face both look at target

Weight is firmly on left foot

BENEFIT The hand action in tennis helps to clarify the action in golf. It begins with a lag of the clubhead, then a release at impact as you accelerate to the finish. This creates clubhead speed and greater ball control.

POINTER DRILL

PROBLEM When you don't hinge your wrists correctly in the golf swing you miss the target because the clubface is not looking directly towards it at impact.

DRILL Attach a tee peg temporarily to the face of a long iron. Insert another one into the back of your golf glove so that it sticks out in front. Adopt the address position and check that both tee pegs are pointing to the target. At the start of the backswing move the shoulders, torso, arms, and club away, then begin to hinge the wrists. When the club reaches hip height the toe looks to the sky; the tee pegs point to the front. At and through impact the tee pegs point to the target; in the forward swing they point to the rear.

FEEL In the backswing you feel the right wrist hinge back on itself as the left one rotates a little. As the left hip clears through impact the wrists release the clubface naturally.

Attach tee peg to clubface

At address, both tee pegs point directly to target

BENEFIT The tee pegs act as a simple but effective visual aid for achieving correct wrist action throughout the golf swing. By learning to hinge the wrists so that they present the clubface square to the target at impact you will send the ball there.

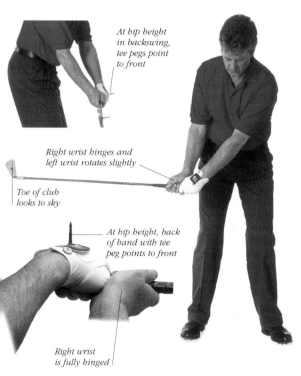

At hip height in backswing, tee pegs point to front

Right wrist hinges and left wrist rotates slightly

Toe of club looks to sky

At hip height, back of hand with tee peg points to front

Right wrist is fully hinged

85

LEFT THUMB UNDER

At top of backswing, wrists are fully cocked and left thumb supports club

Club is on line, with clubhead square to swingpath

PROBLEM Do you miss the target to the right or left? When the clubface is open to its swingpath (looks at the ground) at the top of the backswing the ball misses on the right; when it is closed (looks at the sky) the ball misses on the left.

DRILL Assume a grip with both palms facing each other. Allow the wrists to hinge in the backswing. At the top, check that the left thumb sits under the handle.

Left thumb sits under club handle at top of backswing

FEEL You feel the left thumb supporting the handle and your wrists fully cocked.

Clubhead is square to target

BENEFIT At impact you present the clubface squarely to the target so that your shots reach the mark.

Left thumb is directly under handle

CLOSED CLUBFACE
Clubhead looks upwards;
left thumb is on side of handle.

OPEN CLUBFACE
Clubhead looks downwards;
left thumb is on far side of handle.

SPLIT HANDS

PROBLEM Do you cast the clubhead from the top of the backswing like a fisherman casts a fly? This results in loss of power, poor balance, and misdirected shots.

DRILL Hold the club so that the right hand is at the end of the grip, with part of it on the shaft. Make a backswing to the top.

Backswing feels wider with split hands grip

Left arm extends and right one folds

Left hand sits in usual position

Right one sits further down handle

Then let the arms swing down freely. Your feet initiate the downswing by transferring bodyweight. Your hips rotate to instigate the centrifugal action, which energizes the swing of the arms. The hands and clubhead follow.

FEEL The weight transfer and the swing of the arms feel as if they happen together, but the weight transfers first. The left hand leads the butt of the handle down to the ball. Feel the width created by an extended left arm.

BENEFIT Clubhead speed through impact is achieved when movement in the downswing is from feet to hips, arms, and hands. The clubhead accelerates through the ball, achieving greater distance with less effort.

Right wrist maintains its hinge

Clubhead lags behind weight shift, hip rotation, and swing of arms

SWINGPATH

PROBLEM Do you know that the swingpath of the clubhead should travel 'inside-square-to-inside' of the ball-to-target line but not see or feel this? Without an understanding of the geometry, poor shots will prevail.

DRILL Place a club on the ground. This represents the ball-to-target line. Take hold of another club with both hands, extending your arms forwards. Stand square to the club on the ground so that the two clubs appear in line.

Turn your shoulders as your arms swing up to a half backswing. Keep your eyes on the ground. In your peripheral vision you will see the club shaft track away in an arc. Then let your arms fall freely downwards and up again on the other side. The club in your hands brushes with the ball-to-target line on an arc 'inside-square-to-inside' of it.

FEEL As the arms fall the club feels as if it is swung outwards. As you turn through you feel the arms swinging around and up.

Take up position square to club with arms extended

Clubs look in line with each other

BENEFIT This simple drill helps you to establish a sound muscle memory for the essential geometry of the swing. You will improve your swing – and your scores.

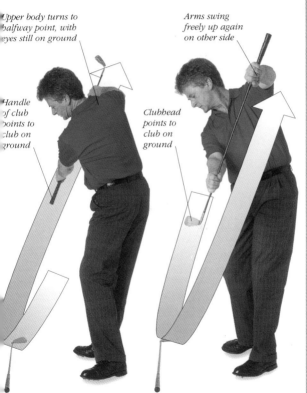

Upper body turns to halfway point, with eyes still on ground

Handle of club points to club on ground

Arms swing freely up again on other side

Clubhead points to club on ground

INSIDE-SQUARE-TO-INSIDE

PROBLEM If you are fearful of hitting the
ball to an obstacle to the right you are likely
to pull the club from 'outside to inside' of
the ball-to-target line. Your efforts to steer
the ball away from the obstacle result in
either a straight pull to the left of the target
or a slice into the obstacle on the right.

Club is on line

*Club
tracks
arc low
to ground
to avoid
balls*

*Shoulders
turn fully*

DRILL Position a semicircle of balls to represent the arc of swing. Make some shots with the object ball. The semicircle of balls should remain intact after each shot.

FEEL The arms swing freely downwards. If you feel your shoulders heave the club down you will scatter the balls.

BENEFIT So long as the clubface is square to the target at impact, the ball will fly straight to the target.

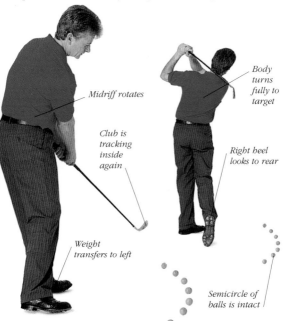

Midriff rotates

Club is tracking inside again

Weight transfers to left

Body turns fully to target

Right heel looks to rear

Semicircle of balls is intact

PLANE OF SWING

PROBLEM Confusion and poor shots arise if your swing action differs according to whether you are using a wood or an iron.

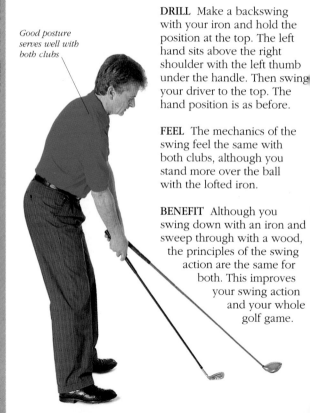

Good posture serves well with both clubs

DRILL Make a backswing with your iron and hold the position at the top. The left hand sits above the right shoulder with the left thumb under the handle. Then swing your driver to the top. The hand position is as before.

FEEL The mechanics of the swing feel the same with both clubs, although you stand more over the ball with the lofted iron.

BENEFIT Although you swing down with an iron and sweep through with a wood, the principles of the swing action are the same for both. This improves your swing action and your whole golf game.

Shaft is on line

Left hand sits above right shoulder

Left hand again sits above right shoulder

Spine angle is slightly more tilted with short iron

Lower body reacts in identical fashion for each club

95

THE CYLINDER

PROBLEM Does your left shoulder rise up in the backswing? Or does it dip down sharply to the ball? Any change in posture once the swing has begun adversely affects the swingpath and angle of attack of the clubface into the ball. This results in errant shots.

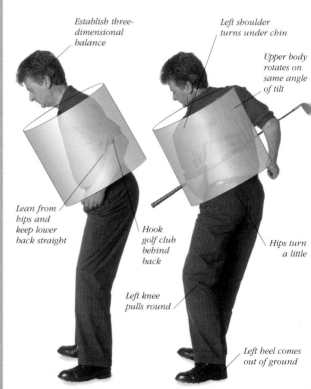

Establish three-dimensional balance

Left shoulder turns under chin

Upper body rotates on same angle of tilt

Lean from hips and keep lower back straight

Hook golf club behind back

Hips turn a little

Left knee pulls round

Left heel comes out of ground

DRILL Hold a club behind your back and lean over from the hips. Make a golf swing by turning first away from and then through to the target without changing the spine's angle of tilt. You will see the handle come around to a point in front of an imaginary ball. Then the clubhead comes down and around to the same point. Make sure that the shaft angle moves on a constant plane. The spine angle is influenced by the length of the club that you are using.

FEEL In the backswing the left shoulder turns easily under the chin. In the forward move feel your feet begin to transfer weight. Your hips turn and your right shoulder moves slightly downwards and under the chin.

BENEFIT The drill helps you to develop a more consistent swingplane. This leads to better contact with the ball and greater accuracy on all shots.

Right shoulder comes down and under chin

Shaft of club returns on same plane

Hips and midriff turn through to target

Right knee points down target line

Right foot is on toes

97

BACK TO THE FENCE

Club is on line at top

PROBLEM Do you thin the ball to the right, hit the ground in front of the ball, or hook it to the left? If so, your swingplane is probably too flat – the arms swing the club around the body on the same plane as the turn of the shoulders.

Left hand sits above right shoulder

Line through elbows sits parallel with ground

DRILL Stand about 30 cm (12 in) from a fence, wall, or hedge. At first, reverse the club in your grip as though striking a ball with the handle. Start by making your backswing in slow motion, taking care not to strike the fence as you continue to the top. Hinge the wrists when they reach about 8 o'clock. Swing through to the end of the swing, avoiding the fence. Gradually build up your speed.

Club swings through ball and up inside ball-to-target line

FEEL You feel that the arms swing up on a steeper plane than the shoulders. At the start of the action you feel that the shoulders, torso, and arms are turning together.

BENEFIT Your angle of attack becomes more appropriate for the club being used. This drill improves the quality and accuracy of shots.

Hips and midriff rotate to face target

Right knee points down target line

Right heel looks to rear

99

TWO CLUBS AND MIRROR

PROBLEM Do your shots have no power despite your swing being too fast? You are snatching the club downwards too quickly at the start of the swing, killing rhythm, tempo, and timing.

Shoulders, midriff, and arms turn together

DRILL Adopt the golf pose in front of a mirror, holding two clubs. Swing back a little, then through. The hands and arms are not strong enough alone. They require the body to rotate and create a free-flowing swing. Increase the fullness of the swing, seeing how little the arms and hands do.

FEEL The clubs feel lighter the more the body turns. Early weight transfer and midriff rotation in the forward move give a sensation of arms swinging down slowly then the clubhead accelerating through the foot of the arc.

Midriff and knees rotate

Feet alter weight shift

BENEFIT Although the hands and arms swing the club to strike the ball, the actions of the larger muscles of the legs, midriff, and body fuel and energize the swing action. You will achieve coordinated movement as well as more power.

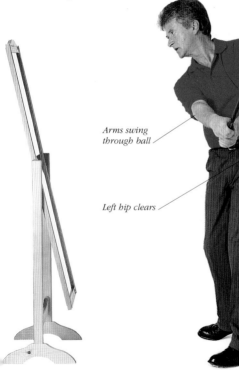

Arms swing through ball

Left hip clears

BACK TO FRONT

PROBLEM Are you so focused on your backswing that you forget to swing the club through the ball? If so, you hit 'at' it rather than 'past' it. This results in a loss of distance and accuracy.

DRILL Go straight to the finish of the golf swing. Hold it. Recognize how your body feels. Then let the arms fall downwards and up into the top of the backswing, turning to accommodate it. Once the club has arrived, swing through to the finish again. Repeat this, holding the finish in a relaxed and balanced way as though posing for the camera.

FEEL You are more aware of the two turns of the body and of the weight transfer. You feel the club accelerate through the imaginary ball to the finish.

Hands sit over left shoulder

Torso points to left of target

Hips look to target, in line with midriff and right knee

Feet are in line with left knee, hips, and shoulder

Arms fall freely downwards

Left thumb sits under handle

Shoulders turn fully so back faces target

Hips turn slightly with left hip coming around

Left heel comes out of ground slightly

BENEFIT Your backswing feels more natural and you are more focused on reaching and holding the end of the swing position. This promotes increased speed through impact and leads to more distance.

103

CLUBHEAD AWARENESS

PROBLEM The club is seldom where it should be during the golf swing. If you have no awareness of the clubhead arriving at the end of the backswing, you will have no feeling of rhythm, tempo, or timing for what is to follow.

DRILL Reverse the club so that you are holding the shaft just below the clubhead. Assume your address position as usual. Swing the club in a smooth, rhythmical way from a full backswing to a complete finish. Then make further swings, holding it the right way round.

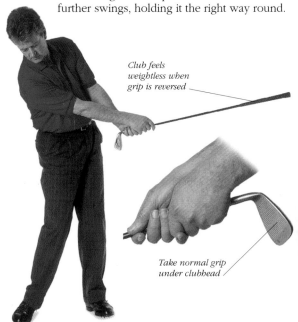

Club feels weightless when grip is reversed

Take normal grip under clubhead

FEEL The reversed club gives a feeling of weightlessness. When you swing with the club the right way round it becomes easy to tell where the clubhead is because you feel its weight. You are immediately aware of the precise moment when the clubhead arrives at the end of the backswing, and you can feel it swish through the ball.

BENEFIT Making a few swings this way at the start of a practice session or a round of golf quickly heightens your awareness of rhythm, tempo, and timing.

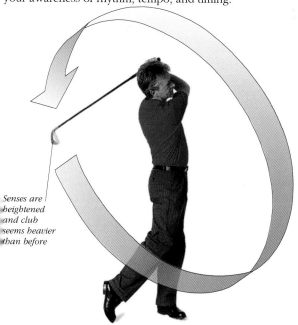

Senses are heightened and club seems heavier than before

FREE FALL

PROBLEM Do you have difficulty in transferring your weight at the start of the forward swing? Does your swing seem to take a lot of effort yet produce little power? If so, you are probably pulling the club downwards with your shoulders as though chopping logs.

DRILL Swing the club to the top of the backswing. Then, keeping the shoulders fully turned, allow the arms to fall freely downwards at the same time as your bodyweight shifts to the left side. The hands separate from the right shoulder as they fall to hip height. Repeat this many times in front of a mirror. Notice how the left arm remains comfortably extended and how the wrists maintain their hinge as the butt of the handle falls downwards.

Hands are above right shoulder

Turn into right side

Bodyweight balanced on right foot

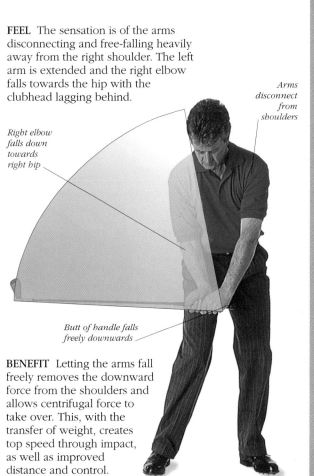

FEEL The sensation is of the arms disconnecting and free-falling heavily away from the right shoulder. The left arm is extended and the right elbow falls towards the hip with the clubhead lagging behind.

Arms disconnect from shoulders

Right elbow falls down towards right hip

Butt of handle falls freely downwards

BENEFIT Letting the arms fall freely removes the downward force from the shoulders and allows centrifugal force to take over. This, with the transfer of weight, creates top speed through impact, as well as improved distance and control.

HIP IT

PROBLEM No matter how hard you try, your friends keep knocking the ball further than you. Your hands and arms are probably doing all the work and cannot generate the necessary clubhead speed through the ball to achieve great distance.

Wrists hinge to point shaft of club to sky

Shoulders and torso turn away from target

Arms swing up to half backswing

Bodyweight moves to right side

DRILL Swing the club to a half backswing. Disconnect the arms from the shoulders, letting them fall downwards with the butt of the club leading the way. Generate power by 'hitting the ball with your hips'. Use a No. 6 or 7 iron at first, to send the ball about 100 m (100 yds). Then use other clubs similarly.

FEEL You feel that the downswing begins with the feet transferring weight; hips rotating to the target; arms following; and hands

Arms swing through, around, and up to full finish

releasing the clubhead through the ball as though 'swishing' it at the last moment. You feel an elasticity of movement, rather than strain.

Midriff rotates to target in powerful way

BENEFIT This drill brings your powerful muscles (feet, knees, hips, and torso) into play. They and the smaller muscles (hands and arms) work in synch to set up the proper order of action and create maximum power with minimum effort.

Bodyweight moves onto left side

BALL UNDER RIGHT FOOT

PROBLEM Are your shots sometimes pulled to the left, whilst at other times to the right? Do you lose your balance on every full swing, with your right knee moving outside your right foot in the backswing, creating a sway and reverse pivot? If so, you have forgotten that the golf swing must be contained within the width of your stance.

DRILL Take up your stance as though playing a shot. Place a ball or a small wedge under your right foot. Make a few swings. The restriction imposed by the ball under your foot prevents the right knee from moving laterally.

FEEL Your first impression is of confinement. Your lower body wants to move laterally but cannot. At the top you are balanced and ready to drive your weight through the ball. The throughswing feels more compact yet irresistible.

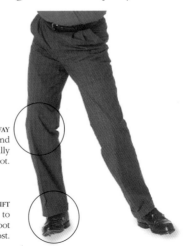

RIGHT KNEE SWAY
Right knee is bent and has moved laterally outside foot.

WEIGHT SHIFT
Weight shifts to outside edge of foot and balance is lost.

BENEFIT This drill makes your upper body better able to turn over the right foot in the backswing in the appropriate coiling action. This sets up the correct order of movement in the forward swing. The result is that your golf swing is a more powerful unit because it is better balanced throughout. The timing becomes more naturally coordinated. More consistent play ensues.

Shoulders turn fully over right foot

Balance points of shoulders, right hip, knee, and foot support each other

Hips turn a little

Wedge golf ball under your right foot

Balance has shifted into right side and remains within feet

111

ADDRESS/IMPACT POSITION

PROBLEM Have you been told to return to the address position at impact? This breaks down the proper order of movement of the forward swing, promoting overactive hand and arm action, and underactive foot and leg work. 'Hooks', 'blocks', and other inconsistent shots result.

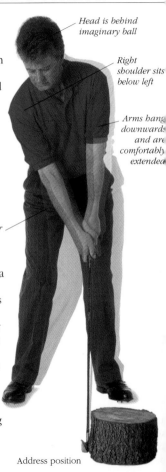

Head is behind imaginary ball

Right shoulder sits below left

Arms hang downwards and are comfortably extended

Balance points of shoulders, hips, knees, and feet support each other

DRILL Set up with your clubhead resting against a log, tree, stone, or other immovable object. At this point you are simply standing as though ready for action. Then make as though to move the object forwards from this standing position. To do so with your hands and arms alone is too much of a strain. Causing the object to move requires input from the big muscles too.

Address position

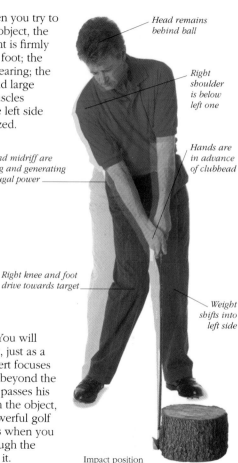

FEEL When you try to move the object, the bodyweight is firmly on the left foot; the hips are clearing; the left arm and large deltoid muscles around the left side are energized.

Head remains behind ball

Right shoulder is below left one

Hips and midriff are clearing and generating centrifugal power

Hands are in advance of clubhead

Right knee and foot drive towards target

Weight shifts into left side

BENEFIT You will realize that, just as a karate expert focuses on a point beyond the object and passes his fist through the object, a more powerful golf shot results when you swing through the ball, not to it.

Impact position

BUNKER DRILLS

Do not be intimidated by the bunker shot: it is easy when you follow basic principles. This is one of the few shots in golf in which the ball and the clubface do not meet. The ball flies off a cushion of sand rather than off the face of the club. The purpose of the swing is to accelerate the clubface through the sand in front of and beneath the ball, maintaining maximum loft on the face.

For open clubface, take conventional hold but with scorelines on clubface looking to right

Align body to left of target

Clubface is open and looks to target

Position ball slightly left of centre

Align shoulders, hips, knees, and feet to left

The right hand and wrist hinge early in the takeaway and remain hinged through the impact zone. This action makes the ball pop up so that it lands softly on the green. Always swing through the sand to a complete finish whenever possible.

Clubface looks directly at target

Different lies require special strategies (see page 118). These pages show the set-up for a conventional 'splash' shot.

Swing club along line of stance, across ball-to-target line

115

TEE PEG

PROBLEM Does the fear of hitting the ball too far make you lose heart? Does your weight end up on the back foot as you attempt to scoop out the ball with a flick of the clubhead and wrists? Do you find bunker shots difficult for this reason? If so, you have forgotten the basic bunker principle that a fully lofted clubface must accelerate through the sand beneath the ball.

Sink tee peg below surface and place ball on top

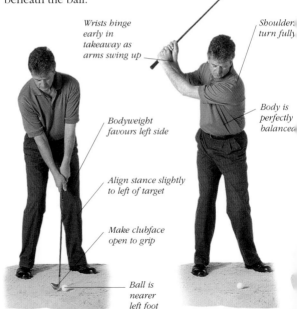

Wrists hinge early in takeaway as arms swing up

Shoulders turn fully

Bodyweight favours left side

Body is perfectly balanced

Align stance slightly to left of target

Make clubface open to grip

Ball is nearer left foot

116

DRILL Push a tee peg into the sand and place a ball on top. Adopt the usual grip and stance, with the ball slightly to the left of centre. Make a swing, aiming to dislodge the tee peg and hit it – not the ball – onto the green. Keep the right wrist hinged backwards as the club enters the sand.

FEEL Your swing feels much longer through the sand. Your hips clear out of the way to enable your arms to swing freely as they lead the clubhead through the sand.

BENEFIT You develop a smoother swing action. The ball floats high and lands on the green.

Focus on dislodging tee peg

Hips clear

Arms lead clubface down and through sand beneath ball

PLUGGED BALL

PROBLEM When faced with a plugged ball, do you panic and your movements become erratic?

DRILL Stand square to the ball-to-target line, with the clubface aligned to target and your bodyweight on the left side. Position the ball back in the stance. Hinge the wrists early as you turn the shoulders, then release them early in the downswing. Aim to get the clubface into the sand behind the ball on a steep angle of attack.

Ball is half-buried in sand

Align body square to target with weight on left side

Right wrist hinges at beginning of backswing

Place ball opposite right foot with clubface square

Settle feet into sand

Hands release clubhead like fisherman casting fly

FEEL The hands and arms feel that they are doing most of the work. Feel the right wrist hinge back on itself as you begin the backswing. Then feel both hands roll the clubface through sand and ball.

BENEFIT This simple technique gives you the confidence and skill to get your plugged ball onto the green.

Hands and arms do the work

Right hand rolls over left one

Toe of club overtakes heel

PLAN B

PROBLEM Are you still trying to scoop the clubhead under the ball with the right hand in an attempt to dig it out, rather than let the clubhead lag into the sand? When all other methods have failed, try this one.

DRILL Stand square but with the ball slightly to left of centre. Grip the club as usual with the left hand but, with the right, hold it in the fingertips and wrap the hand over so that all four knuckles are showing.
Make your swing, letting the wrists

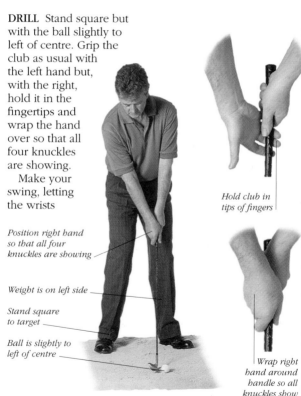

Hold club in tips of fingers

Position right hand so that all four knuckles are showing

Weight is on left side

Stand square to target

Ball is slightly to left of centre

Wrap right hand around handle so all knuckles show

Left wrist is cupped at top of backswing

hinge. As your weight moves into the left side, swish the clubhead into and through the sand.

FEEL As the wrists hinge, the clubface seems to open greatly. The left wrist is cupped and the right palm points down at the top of the backswing.

BENEFIT The strength of the right hand is diffused, and the left arm and hand are free to lag the clubface into the sand. The ball pops up and lands on the green.

Wrists swish clubhead into and through sand

ON-GOING
PRACTICE

The third step to becoming a good golfer is to believe in yourself and your ability, and to know how to maximize your strengths.

HOW TO BELIEVE IN YOURSELF

Hints on using drills and on how to practise have been given on pages 14–18. There is one more vital task to perform on a regular basis before the benefits of your endeavours become evident in your game – you must practise belief in yourself.

○ The subconscious mind is a silent computer that translates every thought into action. 'You are what you think you are', is an old saying that rings true on the golf course.

○ Use your imagination to 'see' a successful end result. Believe that the drills that you have worked on will greatly improve your game.

○ Believe that your game is progressing.

○ Imagine yourself playing each golf shot easily from now on, without the need for too much conscious thought or effort.

○ Avoid using willpower to play well: this suggests that you can't play well without it.

○ Your subconscious does not react to wilful commands – it responds only to your faith and belief in the outcome.

○ As you practise your new skills, affirm to yourself regularly and often how much clearer you are in your mind; how you can feel yourself progressing; how much better you feel about yourself as a golfer. Your behaviour changes, as does your mood. You find yourself doing the right things without having to think about them. Suddenly things begin to work out for you.

○ When you have a feeling of success, you will have success.

○ Simply know that you are now a better player.

○ Do not underestimate the power of this affirmative mental process.

SELF-AFFIRMATION
A good golfing technique needs to be supported by a firm belief in yourself in order to make you perform well on the golf course.

How to Lower your Scores

A strong mental attitude, as well as technical skill, is required when playing golf. All expert players use their sense of reasoning on the golf course. Here are some ways to keep your mind focused when competing:

○ It is impossible to hit good shots on the golf course if you are thinking about your technique. Play golf – negotiate the ball from A to B in the most economical way possible. Save working on your technique for the practice ground.

○ Give every hole a plan and every shot a realistic target. Make your targets big ones – they are easier to hit and give you confidence.

○ Never compare yourself to any other player – you are a unique golfer, with your own style, strengths, experience, and par. Keep to your game plan within these parameters.

○ Always play the course – never your opponent – for the same reasons.

○ Play to your strengths, using the clubs that work best for you, whenever possible. Save working on your weaknesses until you are off the course.

○ Utilize the teeing area to suit your shape of shot. If, for example, your drives normally set off to the left before bending to the right, tee off from the right side of the teeing area, making your landing area bigger.

○ Keep in the present tense by dealing with each shot honestly and leaving the next shot until later. You cannot hit a good shot if you are preoccupied with the next one.

○ Don't count your score until the end and avoid the 'all I have to do' syndrome.

○ Be patient – particularly with yourself. No player hits bad shots on purpose – accidents happen even to the best player.

TACTICAL PLAY
Once you have mastered golfing techniques, learn to play tactically on the golf course so that you can maximize your strengths.

GLOSSARY

ball-to-target line The imaginary line between the ball and the target.

block A shot that sets off to the right of the target, caused by a lateral slide.

closed clubface Clubface is aligned to the left of its swingpath.

closed stance Body is aligned to the right of the target line.

draw A mild right-to-left flight of the ball.

fade A mild left-to-right flight of the ball.

hook A ball that sets off to the right of target but bends severely to the left in flight.

inside-square-to-inside The arc of swing that brushes with, and remains on the near side of, the ball-to-target line.

muscle memory The ability to repeat a movement automatically, without conscious thought.

object ball The ball to be played when, in practice, other balls act as decoys.

off line When the ball or the clubface is pulled off the intended line of flight.

on line When the ball or the clubface is direct to target.

open clubface Clubface is aligned to the right of its swingpath.

open stance Body is aligned to the left of the target line.

reverse pivot When the bodyweight remains on the left foot at the top of the backswing.

sweetspot The area of the clubface – usually the centre – that produces the perfect flight or roll.

thin To strike the ball by the bottom edge of the blade, usually on the upswing, causing it to shoot along the ground, out of control.

ACKNOWLEDGMENTS

Thanks to Mark Tattam for his design assistance.
The author is indebted to the Tommy Armour Golf Co. (Scotland) Ltd. for their support in providing equipment and Mark Scot golf shirts.